DATE DUE

PRINTED IN U.S.A.

A PERSPECTIVES
FLIP BOOK

The Split History of the
AMERICAN REVOLUTION

BRITISH PERSPECTIVE

BY MICHAEL BURGAN

CONTENT CONSULTANT:
Lawrence Babits, PhD
Professor Emeritus, Department of History
East Carolina University

COMPASS POINT BOOKS
a capstone imprint

About the Author:

Michael Burgan has written numerous books for children and young adults during his nearly 20 years as a freelance writer. Many of his books have focused on U.S. history, geography, and the lives of world leaders. Michael has won several awards for his writing. He lives in Santa Fe, New Mexico, with his cat, Callie.

Source Notes:

Patriot Perspective

Page 9, line 9: Old South Meeting House. 20 April 2012. www.oldsouthmeetinghouse.org/osmh_123456789files/BostonTeaPartyBegan. aspx#december161773

Page 11, line 2: Henry Steele Commager and Richard B. Morris, eds. *The Spirit of Seventy-Six: The Story of the American Revolution As Told by Participants.* New York: Da Capo Press, 1995, p. 81.

Page 13, line 6: Ibid., p. 129.

Page 15, line 4: Ibid., p. 314.

Page 21, line 1: Ibid., p. 595.

Page 22, line 1: Ibid., p. 642.

Page 24, line 9: South Carolina Loyalists in the American Revolution. 20 April 2012. www.clemson.edu/caah/cedp/cudp/pubs/lambert/lambert.pdf 141

Page 26, line 6: *Spirit of Seventy-Six: The Story of the American Revolution As Told by Participants,* p. 1122.

Page 26, sidebar, line 7: African American Lives. 20 April 2012. www.wps.ablongman.com/long_carson_aal_1/27/6981/1787151.cw/index.html

Page 28, line 5: *Spirit of Seventy-Six: The Story of the American Revolution As Told by Participant,* p. 1241.

Page 29, line 9: Robert Middlekauf. *The Glorious Cause: The American Revolution 1763–1789.* New York: Oxford University Press, 1982, p. 596.

British Perspective

Page 4, line 8: History Today—The Coronation of George III. 20 April 2012. www.historytoday.com/richard-cavendish/coronation-george-iii

Page 6, line 2: Digital History. 20 April 2012. www.digitalhistory.uh.edu/documents/documents_p2.cfm?doc=247

Page 9, sidebar, line 4: Thomas J Fleming. *Liberty!: The American Revolution.* New York: Viking, 1997, pages 50–51.

Page 12, line 2: *Spirit of Seventy-Six: The Story of the American Revolution As Told by Participants,* p. 71.

Page 13, line 8: Ibid., p. 97.

Page 14, line 4: Massachusetts Historical Society. 20 April 2012. www.masshist.org/bh/wallerp2text.html.

Page 17, line 22: *Spirit of Seventy-Six: The Story of the American Revolution As Told by Participants,* p. 524.

Page 21, line 16: Christopher Hibbert. *Redcoats and Rebels: The American Revolution Through British Eyes.* New York: Norton, 1990, p. 201–202.

Page 29, line 8: Stanley Weintraub. *Iron Tears: America's Battle for Freedom, Britain's Quagmire: 1775–1783.* New York: Free Press, 2005, p. 304.

Table of Contents

4
CHAPTER 1
DEALING WITH REBELS

11
CHAPTER 2
A DISTANT WAR

18
CHAPTER 3
SUCCESSES AND FAILURES

23
CHAPTER 4
THE WAR IS LOST

30
INDEX

SHARED RESOURCES

I
GLOSSARY
INTERNET SITES

II
TIMELINE

III
SELECT BIBLIOGRAPHY
FURTHER READING

DEALING WITH REBELS

*O*nly 22 years old, George III was about to be crowned king of one of the world's great empires. It was September 22, 1761, and the military that George inherited with the lands of Great Britain had helped build that empire. Just a year before, British troops defeated French forces in Canada. And in the year to come, George's military would win victories against Spain in Cuba and the Philippines. British influence in India was on the rise. George said with pride, "I glory in the name of Britain."

Britain's long war against Spain, France, and other European nations, called the French and Indian War in North America, finally ended in 1763. The British greatly expanded their holdings in North America, adding to their 13 colonies along the Atlantic coast.

George III became king after the death of his grandfather George II.

TAXING THE COLONIES

One of George's concerns was keeping peace with the American Indian tribes along the frontier. American colonists had been moving onto Indian lands, and Indian relations with British officials had recently soured. War broke out in 1763 as the Indians attacked British forts in the west.

George issued a proclamation that said American colonists could not settle west of the Appalachian Mountains. The Proclamation of 1763 limited who could trade with the Indians in that region. The king and his aides also planned to send as many as 10,000 additional troops to the American frontier. To help pay the costs, Parliament passed the Sugar Act in 1764. The law raised some taxes on the colonies. It also called for collecting taxes, known as duties, that were already in place. The colonists had avoided paying the earlier duties by smuggling goods into the colonies.

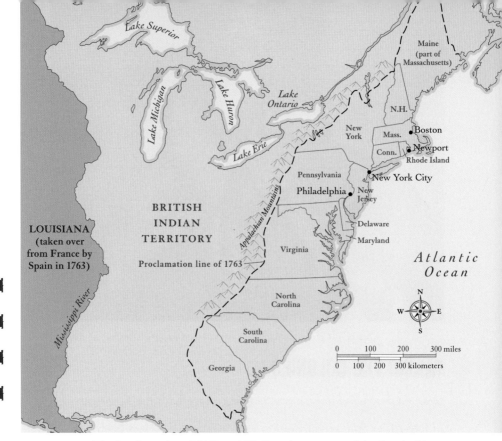

The Proclamation of 1763 prohibited settlement west of the Appalachians.

In the Proclamation of 1763, George called the Americans his "loving subjects." The Americans, though, did not love the Sugar Act, and some spoke out against it.

George's need for money outweighed any concern about American liberty. Parliament passed the Stamp Act of 1765, which called for a tax on printed documents. This time the colonists did more than grumble. Colonists in several cities protested. Many also boycotted British goods. The boycott angered British merchants, who lost money because of it.

Parliament repealed the Stamp Act in 1766. But the need for more money from the colonies had not gone away.

Leading the fight against the tax policies were American colonists known as Patriots. The Patriots claimed the only fair taxes were ones passed by elected colonial officials. Since the colonists had no voting representatives in Parliament, Patriots believed Parliament had no right to tax them. British leaders argued back that the Americans had "virtual representation." They said that members of Parliament did what was best for the empire as a whole, and the Americans had to accept their actions.

Parliament quickly carried out its plan to keep taxing the colonists. The Townshend Acts of 1767 taxed such items as lead, paint, glass, and tea. In the colonies the new taxes led to more boycotts but no real violence—except in Boston. British officials sparked the protests after they seized a local merchant's ship. After the protest ended, British Governor Francis Bernard of Massachusetts asked the British to send troops to Boston. The first of these Regulars, as the soldiers were called, arrived in September 1768.

BOSTON RIOT

From the beginning the British soldiers were met with hostility by many Boston residents. Soldiers were insulted or beaten on the streets. These actions angered the soldiers, who only wanted to be let alone to do their jobs. Some retaliated by harassing the colonists.

On the night of March 5, 1770, things came to a head. In front of the Customs House, a crowd of people were yelling and throwing rocks, sticks, and icy snowballs at several soldiers. Someone yelled,

British soldiers soon grew weary of abuse from Bostonians.

"Fire!" which the soldiers took as an order, firing on the crowd. Five Boston residents died, and six others were wounded.

Eight soldiers and their captain, Thomas Preston, were arrested and tried for murder. Ironically, Patriot lawyers John Adams and Josiah Quincy Jr. represented the soldiers. Preston and six soldiers were acquitted. The two soldiers found guilty of manslaughter were branded on their thumbs and sent back to England. The verdict did little to ease the tension between the Regulars and the colonists.

THE TEA ACT

As the American boycott went on, British merchants again demanded a repeal of taxes on the colonies. In 1770 King George's advisers met to discuss the issue. Some said Parliament should repeal all the taxes except one on tea. The king agreed.

The repeal of the other taxes seemed to satisfy many Americans, and the colonies were mostly calm until 1773. That year Parliament decided to help the East India Company, which imported tea from India to Great Britain. The Tea Act lowered the tax on tea and gave the company the sole right to sell tea in the colonies. British leaders thought the colonists would be happy with the act, because it allowed them to pay much less for tea than they had previously. But many colonists saw it as interference. Boston Patriots responded by throwing several hundred crates of East India tea into the harbor.

The "Boston Tea Party" infuriated King George and Lord Frederick North, the prime minister. The two men agreed that Massachusetts had to be punished. George shut down Boston harbor and limited local government power there. The king also

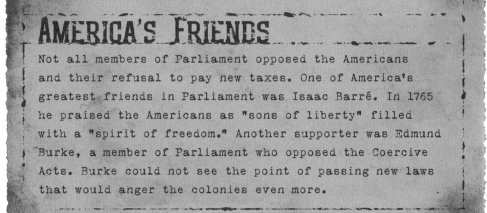

AMERICA'S FRIENDS

Not all members of Parliament opposed the Americans and their refusal to pay new taxes. One of America's greatest friends in Parliament was Isaac Barré. In 1765 he praised the Americans as "sons of liberty" filled with a "spirit of freedom." Another supporter was Edmund Burke, a member of Parliament who opposed the Coercive Acts. Burke could not see the point of passing new laws that would anger the colonies even more.

sent more troops to Boston. The British called these and other measures the Coercive Acts. They were meant to coerce the colonists to obey the king and Parliament.

Lord North advised King George to deal firmly with the Americans.

To carry out the new laws and restore order, George named General Thomas Gage the governor of Massachusetts. Gage had served in America for many years and had an American wife. George trusted his view of the colonists. Gage believed the Americans would not respect the British if the king allowed the colonists to do what they wanted.

The Coercive Acts, though, did not end the protests in America. The other colonies united behind Massachusetts, and all but Georgia sent delegates to the First Continental Congress in September 1774. The Congress stated that the colonists were still loyal to King George, but they opposed policies that denied them their freedom and rights.

Back in Britain merchants suffered as the Americans once again stopped buying their goods. But this time King George refused to give in and repeal the laws. To him, the New England colonists were now rebels. Before long all the Americans who challenged him would be.

A DISTANT WAR
CH. 2

By fall 1774 many Massachusetts militia members were already preparing to fight. In spring 1775 General Gage decided to stop the rebels. On the night of April 18, about 700 of his men left Boston for Concord, Massachusetts, to destroy the gunpowder and weapons stored there. But American spies knew about the march, and word quickly spread to neighboring towns.

Early the next morning, Lieutenant John Barker and the Regulars with him saw armed militiamen waiting for them in Lexington. Someone fired a shot—Barker was sure it was a

British soldiers marched to Concord to destroy gunpowder and weapons.

colonist. The Regulars fired in return. Barker and the other officers ordered their men to stop, but "the men were so wild they could hear no orders." Finally the British marched on, leaving eight dead Americans behind them.

At 8 a.m. the British force reached Concord. The soldiers found just a small amount of rebel supplies before more firing erupted. Several British soldiers were killed, and the rest retreated toward Boston. More rebels poured through the trees and over the hills to join in the attack. British reinforcements from Boston helped Barker and the Regulars get back to camp, but not before dozens were killed.

Word of Lexington and Concord reached London almost six weeks later. Some British citizens feared that battling the colonists could leave Britain open to attacks by France or Spain. But George was determined to press hard on the rebels, believing that once they "have felt a smart blow, they will submit."

BUNKER HILL

General Gage hoped that smart blow would come just outside Boston. By mid-June the British there were surrounded by thousands of rebel militia. But several hills outside the city were not defended. Gage hoped to seize the hills and use them to attack the Americans. He had recently received more troops, as well as three new generals—William Howe, Henry Clinton, and John Burgoyne. Each would play key roles in the battles to come.

The attack was scheduled for June 18. Late the night of June 16, General Clinton heard noises on a distant hill. Sunrise the next morning would reveal the source of that sound—Americans digging feverishly to build a redoubt before the British could attack. The small fort went up on Breed's Hill, but the fighting that soon began was called the Battle of Bunker Hill.

General Howe led the first wave of British soldiers. Weighed down by their heavy backpacks and supplies, the troops were shot by the Americans stationed at the redoubt and behind stone walls.

British soldiers fought in organized formation during the Battle of Bunker Hill.

Clinton soon arrived with more men. Also fighting was Lieutenant John Waller, a British Marine. He prepared his men for a charge as the rebel guns fired all around them. The British attacked the redoubt from all sides with their bayonets. Waller saw the redoubt "streaming with blood and strewed with dead and dying men."

The bravery of Waller and others forced the Americans to flee. But the British victory at Bunker Hill came at a high price — more than 1,000 casualties, almost half of the men who fought that day. The news of the deaths and injuries stirred action in London. George and his advisers knew they needed a much bigger army. They hired Hessian troops from small kingdoms in Germany.

George also removed General Gage from his command, hoping Howe would take bolder action. Finally George officially declared that the colonies were in a state of rebellion, and the rebels were traitors to the crown.

VICTORY IN NEW YORK

The king and his generals decided New York, with its larger harbor, offered a better position for carrying out attacks to either the north or south. And it had more Loyalists than the rebel stronghold of Boston. Making the move, however, required more ships. The British did not leave Boston until March 1776. Howe went to Nova Scotia, Canada, before heading to New York. The Americans under George Washington left for New York as well.

The British were preparing for the largest overseas invasion in their history. Bunker Hill had convinced them that the Americans were more than unskilled farmers causing trouble. The Americans' declaration of independence in July 1776 confirmed it.

That summer about 35,000 British troops began massing on Staten Island. British Admiral Lord Richard Howe joined his brother, General William Howe, in New York. The Howes were preparing for war, but at the same time, London had given them the power to discuss surrender terms and possible pardons for the rebels. The brothers sent a message to George Washington to set up a meeting. Washington said he had no power to discuss political issues. The fighting would go on.

The British defeated the Americans at the Battle of Long Island.

British and Hessian troops began crossing over to Long Island August 22. William Howe hoped to go from there to Manhattan, the heart of New York City. But General Clinton came up with the plan for the Battle of Long Island. Scouting on horseback, Clinton saw a pass that would let the British sneak up on the Americans waiting for them in Brooklyn. British troops attacked the Americans from the front August 27, while Clinton led his men through the pass. The British had almost 400 casualties. But the Americans had at least 1,000, with 1,000 more taken prisoner.

With the battle won, the Howes once again tried to talk peace. In September Lord Richard Howe met with three members of the Continental Congress, John Adams, Benjamin Franklin, and

Edward Rutledge. Howe said King George was willing to grant pardons to the Americans if they would give up their quest for independence. But the Americans refused.

A NEW YEAR

By November General William Howe had pushed some of Washington's force into New Jersey after taking several thousand more prisoners. Meanwhile, Howe sent a small force under Lord Charles Cornwallis to pursue the rebels. But Howe was content to hold off a major battle until the next year. He knew General Washington's forces had shrunk greatly, and the remaining soldiers were losing hope.

To provide food for his troops for the winter, General Howe set up posts near the rich farmland of northern New Jersey. He then left for New York City. Several days after Christmas, Howe received bad news. On the morning of December 26, Washington had launched a daring raid on Trenton, which was held by a Hessian force. Hundreds of the German soldiers were killed or taken prisoner. Cornwallis, who had left New Jersey, was ordered back to confront the rebels. But early in January the rebels scored another victory at Princeton.

Howe did not seem overly troubled by the losses. But Colonel William Harcourt wrote home his own thoughts. He placed some blame on Howe for stationing the troops where he did. And the Americans, he said, "are now become a formidable enemy."

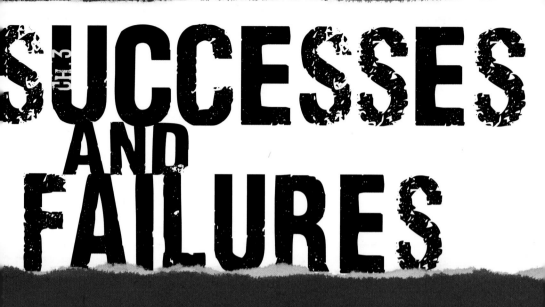

SUCCESSES AND FAILURES

Back in London some members of Parliament still opposed the war. But most lawmakers supported King George and the war effort. Confidence remained high even as rumors reached the city that the French were preparing for war. France, the British knew, was already sending supplies to the rebels.

In New York General William Howe made plans for his next campaign—an attack on the rebel capital of Philadelphia. In July 1777 Howe put about 15,000 men on ships and left New York to sail into Chesapeake Bay. The forces landed in northern Maryland

and then began their march toward Philadelphia. The first action of the campaign came September 11 at Brandywine Creek in Pennsylvania. Howe split his forces, attacking with a smaller force from the front while sending a larger force to circle around the Americans and attack from the rear. The Americans suffered heavy losses. By the end of September, Howe's men triumphantly entered Philadelphia.

General William Howe led the British forces in the colonies.

Many of the British troops were based in nearby Germantown. In early October Howe heard the noise of battle and rode to investigate. He saw some of his men retreating. "For shame, light infantry," the general called. "I never saw you retreat before." Howe thought his men faced only an American scouting party. Instead, Washington had launched a major attack from several directions.

Some British forces took cover in a stone house close to the main British camp. They held off the Americans long enough for reinforcements to arrive. The battle was fought in a thick fog, adding to the smoke from the cannons. In the confusion some

British soldiers took cover in the Chew house during the Battle of Germantown.

Americans fired at their own troops. Despite suffering more than 500 casualties, the British troops beat back the American attack.

SARATOGA

At almost the same time, several hundred miles away, John Burgoyne was trying to avoid a disaster. Burgoyne had started his campaign from Canada with high spirits, boosted by a quick victory at Fort Ticonderoga in July. But that success was quickly followed by a defeat outside Bennington, Vermont. Adding to his problems, Burgoyne found it harder to get supplies the farther he went from Canada. The large number of Loyalist forces he expected to join his army never appeared. And Burgoyne was still counting on help from General Howe—not realizing it would never come.

Meanwhile, an American army under Horatio Gates was gathered outside Saratoga, waiting for Burgoyne. The British troops were confident of victory. The Americans, though, did not run when the two armies met September 19. Burgoyne's army gained control of the area, but suffered twice as many casualties as the Americans.

In the following weeks, Burgoyne saw American sharpshooters pick off his troops and watched his food supplies shrink. He learned that some of Clinton's troops were heading north from New York. Burgoyne hoped he could meet up with Clinton, but his men would have to fight their way out of Saratoga. He made a desperate attack October 7 on the larger American forces.

The Americans swarmed ahead and captured British artillery. Over the next several days, more rebel reinforcements reached Saratoga. Burgoyne knew he was defeated. He surrendered to Gates with almost 6,000 of his men.

WHAT NEXT?

The news from Saratoga jolted the king and his aides. "You cannot conquer America," Parliament member Lord Chatham told his fellow lawmakers. "If I were an American ... while a foreign troop was landed in my country, I never would lay down my arms— never! Never! Never!"

The report from Saratoga also stirred the French. In February 1778 they signed a treaty of alliance with the Americans. Spain would later side with the Americans as well. King George prepared to fight France, his country's longtime enemy. General Clinton

Burgoyne's surrender at Saratoga was a major blow to the British.

replaced William Howe as the commander in the colonies, and the British forces in Philadelphia were sent to New York.

The news from France also inspired thousands of British men to join the military. Meanwhile, three British officials traveled to Philadelphia to offer peace one last time. They were Frederick Howard, Earl of Carlisle; William Eden; and George Johnstone. The men promised if the Americans rejected independence, the British would pull out all of their troops, grant free trade, and allow American representatives in Parliament, among other things. But the rebels refused the offer. The war would go on, with the British now facing a much larger and more powerful enemy.

THE WAR IS LOST

CH.4

With the failure of the peace talks, the British pursued a new plan. The fighting would shift to the southern colonies, where the British counted on military aid from Loyalists.

Clinton sent a force of 3,500 soldiers to Georgia. The capital, Savannah, fell to the British at the end of 1778, and soon the whole colony came under royal control. The next British target was Charleston, South Carolina. Clinton led another force there at the end of 1779 and prepared for a siege that began the next February. The siege lasted several weeks, with both sides turning cannons on each other. American commander Benjamin Lincoln surrendered May 12. About 5,000 Americans were taken prisoner.

WAR IN THE CAROLINAS

After taking Charleston, Clinton returned to New York, leaving Lord Cornwallis in charge of the Carolina forces. Reporting to Cornwallis was cavalry officer Banastre Tarleton. At Waxhaws, an area near the North Carolina border, Tarleton gave rebel commander Abraham Buford a chance to surrender before the British attacked. Buford refused.

The hard-charging British cavalry stunned the Americans. Some rebels tried to surrender, but Tarleton and his men fought on.

Riding with Tarleton were Loyalist troops. Loyalists guarded newly built forts, and at times the only British on the battlefield were officers guiding Loyalist forces. The knowledge of local Americans also helped in preparing for battle. In August 1780 Cornwallis faced a large rebel force at Camden, South Carolina. His Loyalist sources told him how to take advantage of swamps in the area. Cornwallis' infantry began the attack, and the cavalry finished off the Americans. The rebels quickly fled, but not before suffering almost 2,000 casualties.

South Carolina seemed to be firmly under British control, although rebel raiders did cause trouble. France and Spain had not yet been able to give the Americans effective help. They were more concerned with acquiring British lands in other parts of the world.

The British scored a victory at Camden, South Carolina, in 1780.

Cornwallis next moved into North Carolina, but he didn't stay long. Behind him a rebel force surrounded Loyalist troops at Kings Mountain, South Carolina. The Americans fired from behind trees and ran for cover whenever the British charged. The British had about 300 men dead or wounded and another 700 captured. The Americans had fewer than 100 casualties. The loss forced Cornwallis to retreat from North Carolina.

Back in South Carolina by the end of October, Cornwallis and his men suffered miserably. Food and medical supplies were hard to find. The men wore ragged clothes and slept in log huts. Meanwhile, across South Carolina, Loyalist support seemed to shrink as the rebels grew stronger. Cornwallis set up camp for several months, planning another assault on North Carolina.

CAROLINA LOSSES

The year 1781 began with bad news for Cornwallis. He had sent out Tarleton to hunt for a rebel force led by Daniel Morgan. The American set up a defense at a spot in South Carolina called the Cowpens. Tarleton, as usual, quickly thrust his men into battle, expecting the Americans to retreat. Instead, Morgan expertly moved his infantry and cavalry to hold off each British attack. Realizing they were defeated, most of the British surrendered, although Tarleton managed to escape.

Cornwallis set off after the Americans, chasing them into North Carolina. Hoping to move quickly, he left behind his tents and most of his supply wagons. American soldiers had been through the area already, picking it clean of supplies. The lack of available food weakened Cornwallis' army.

By March 1781 the American force in the Carolinas numbered around 4,500, about double the number of Cornwallis' troops. Led by General Nathanael Greene, the rebels made a stand at Guilford Courthouse. The Americans set up three lines of defense, as they had at the Cowpens. Cornwallis had his horse shot out from under him. He took another and rode dangerously close to the enemy lines. A sergeant took hold of the horse, warning the general that he was in danger of being captured or killed.

Cornwallis made it back safely to his troops, but the battle did not go well. At one point the general ordered his artillery to fire grapeshot—tiny metal balls packed into a shell. The shot was designed to cut down many soldiers at once, but with soldiers packed so close together, Regulars as well as rebels took the hits. The British finally forced the Americans to flee, but suffered many casualties.

By April Cornwallis was thinking of taking his men to Virginia. He wanted to defeat the rebels there because from Virginia, the Americans could supply their forces to the south. And as long as the rebels fought effectively in the Carolinas, the British would never gain the full support of the residents there.

Clinton had been thinking about Virginia too. A British force under Benedict Arnold had arrived there in December 1780. They destroyed supplies and generally created terror. Another 4,200 British troops soon followed them, and when Cornwallis arrived in the spring, he brought about 1,500 more.

General Cornwallis scored a costly win at the Battle of Guilford Courthouse.

LAST GASP

Cornwallis had acted on his own in leaving the Carolinas for Virginia. Clinton feared that leaving the region would expose Charleston and Georgia to rebel attacks. As 1781 went on, the two generals exchanged letters, with Cornwallis growing upset with Clinton's requests. In June Clinton asked Cornwallis to send troops to New York because he feared an attack there. Another letter told Cornwallis to plan a raid on Philadelphia, but then Clinton told him to forget that plan. Finally Clinton told him to build a base in Virginia that could serve as a port for the British navy. Cornwallis did so at Yorktown.

Back in New York, Clinton worried about the Americans' plans. The attack on New York that he feared never came. Instead, a note from Cornwallis sent August 31 told the story: "There are between 30 and 40 sail within the capes, mostly ships of war, and some of them very large." A French naval fleet had reached Virginia. A small rebel land force was also nearby. Fearing heavy losses if he decided to fight his way out, Cornwallis decided to stay. He counted on reinforcements from Clinton to help him escape.

Clinton did send warships to confront the French. But the warships didn't repel the French fleet. And the only troops that reached Virginia were a combined American and French force of more than 10,000. Cornwallis was outnumbered, with no way to escape. In late September the rebels began a siege of Yorktown that lasted several weeks. By October 9 rebel cannons pounded the British positions, and the Americans seized two redoubts.

Cornwallis knew he had lost and made the decision to surrender. At the surrender ceremony October 19, Cornwallis said he didn't feel well enough to attend, sending General Charles O'Hara in his place. As O'Hara led the defeated soldiers away, their band played the song "The World Turned Upside Down." The song expressed what the soldiers must have felt—shock that their great army had lost to a group of rebels.

In late November news of the defeat reached London. Lord North threw out his arms and shouted, "O God! It is all over!" But King George was not ready to quit. Early in 1782 Clinton received word that the war would continue—but without any additional reinforcements.

George, however, was increasingly alone in wanting to fight on. Many members of Parliament were tired of spending money and losing men on what seemed a lost cause. The British and Americans began peace talks. When the Treaty of Paris was signed September 3, 1783, George had to accept the loss of this distant, rich part of his empire.

George remained king of Great Britain until 1820, although mental illness made him less active in government for most of those years. George had tried to assert his power, believing that his father and grandfather had given too much control to Parliament. But in the end his actions not only lost the American colonies, they also gave even more power to Parliament.

INDEX

Adams, John, 8, 16
American Indians, 5
Arnold, Benedict, 27

Barker, John, 11–12, 13
Barré, Isaac, 9
battles
    Bennington, 20
    Brandywine, 19
    Bunker Hill, 13–14, 15
    Camden, 24
    Cowpens, the, 26
    Fort Ticonderoga, 20
    Germantown, 19–20
    Guilford Courthouse,
      26, 27
    Kings Mountain, 25
    Lexington and Concord,
      11–13
    Long Island, 16
    Princeton, 17
    Saratoga, 21
    Trenton, 17
    Yorktown, 28–29
Bernard, Francis, 7
Boston Riot, 7–8
Boston Tea Party, 9
boycotts, 6, 7, 9, 10
Burgoyne, John, 13, 20–21

Canada, 4, 15, 20
Charleston, siege of, 23–24
Chatham, Lord, 21
Clinton, Henry, 13, 14, 16, 21–22,
    23, 24, 27, 28, 29
Continental Congress, 10, 16
Cornwallis, Lord Charles, 17,
    24, 25, 26–29

declaration of independence, 15

East India Company, 9
Eden, William, 22

French and Indian War, 4

Gage, Thomas, 10, 11, 13, 15
George III, King, 4, 5, 6, 9–10,
    13, 14–15, 17, 18, 21, 29

Harcourt, William, 17
Hessian soldiers, 14, 16, 17
Howard, Frederick, 22
Howe, Richard, 15, 16–17
Howe, William, 13, 15, 16, 17,
    18–19, 20, 22

Johnstone, George, 22

laws
    Coercive Acts, 9–10
    Proclamation of 1763, 5–6
    Stamp Act, 6
    Sugar Act, 5, 6
    Tea Act, 9
    Townshend Acts, 7
Loyalists, 15, 20, 23, 24, 25

North, Lord Frederick, 9, 29

O'Hara, Charles, 29

Parliament, 5, 6, 7, 9, 10, 18,
    21, 22, 29
Preston, Thomas, 8

Quincy, Josiah Jr., 8

surrender, 15, 21, 24, 26, 29

Tarleton, Banastre, 24, 26
taxes, 5, 6–7, 9
Treaty of Paris, 29

Waller, John, 14
Washington, George, 15, 17, 19

The Split History of the
AMERICAN REVOLUTION

PATRIOT PERSPECTIVE

BY MICHAEL BURGAN

CONTENT CONSULTANT:
Lawrence Babits, PhD
Professor Emeritus, Department of History
East Carolina University

COMPASS POINT BOOKS
a capstone imprint

Compass Point Books
1710 Roe Crest Drive
North Mankato, Minnesota 56003
www.capstonepub.com

Library of Congress Cataloging-in-Publication Data
Burgan, Michael.
The split history of the American Revolution : a perspectives flip book / by Michael Burgan.
pages cm. — (Perspectives flip book)
Includes bibliographical references and index.
Summary: "Describes the opposing viewpoints of the British and Patriots during the American Revolution."— Provided by publisher.
ISBN 978-0-7565-4570-3 (library binding)
ISBN 978-0-7565-4592-5 (paperback)
ISBN 978-0-7565-4629-8 (ebook PDF)
1. United States — History — Revolution, 1775-1783 — Juvenile literature. I. Title.
E208.B94 2013
973.3—dc23
                                                            2012004681

EDITOR
ANGIE KAELBERER

DESIGNER
ASHLEE SUKER

MEDIA RESEARCHER
WANDA WINCH

LIBRARY CONSULTANT
KATHLEEN BAXTER

PRODUCTION SPECIALIST
MICHELLE BIEDSCHEID

IMAGE CREDITS

Patriot Perspective: Alamy: North Wind Picture Archives, 5, 19, 29, Corbis, cover (top), 11; Courtesy of Army Art Collection, U.S. Army Center of Military History, 13, 20, 25; Getty Images Inc: Stock Montage, 8; Library of Congress: Prints and Photographs Division, cover (bottom), 22; National Archives and Records Administration, 16; Newscom: akg images, 15

British Perspective: Alamy: North Wind Picture Archives, 5, 8, 10, 14, 16, 25; Anne S. K. Brown Military Collection, Brown University Library, 19; Bridgeman Art Library International/Delaware Art Museum, Wilmington, USA/Howard Pyle, 20; Corbis, cover (bottom); "Hoskins House" by Dale Gallon, image courtesy of Gallon Historical Art, Gettysburg, Pa., 27; Library of Congress: Prints and Photographs Division, cover (top): National Park Service, Harpers Ferry Center/Lloyd Kenneth Townsend, artist, 12; SuperStock Inc: SuperStock, 22

Art elements Shutterstock: Color Symphony, paper texture; Ektkar, flag; Sandra Cunningham, grunge photo, SvetlanaR, grunge lines

Printed in the United States of America in Stevens Point, Wisconsin.
042012   006678WZF12

Table of Contents

4

CHAPTER 1

THE ROAD TO WAR

12

CHAPTER 2

A WAR FOR INDEPENDENCE

18

CHAPTER 3

DIFFICULT YEARS

24

CHAPTER 4

FINAL VICTORY

30

INDEX

SHARED RESOURCES

I

GLOSSARY
INTERNET SITES

II

TIMELINE

III

SELECT BIBLIOGRAPHY
FURTHER READING

THE ROAD TO WAR

*I*t was August 14, 1765. Across Boston several thousand angry

people poured out into the streets. Shouts of "Liberty, property,

and no stamps!" filled the air. The marchers were furious about

the Stamp Act, a new law that taxed paper goods and documents

of all kinds. That night enraged protesters burned a straw effigy of

Andrew Oliver, the unlucky local official picked to collect the taxes.

The mob also tore down a building Oliver owned and then headed

to his home and wrecked furniture there. More destruction followed

in the days to come.

Patriots protested the Stamp Act by demonstrating and hanging effigies.

The Stamp Act of 1765 was part of a new policy for the 13 American colonies—one that drove many colonists to protest British rule. Leading the fight against the policy were American colonists known as Patriots. They challenged British efforts to raise taxes and squash the colonists' freedoms. The Patriots' ideas and actions put the colonies and Great Britain on the road to war.

A CHANGING RELATIONSHIP

Until the 1760s Parliament and the British crown paid little attention to the distant American colonies—and most Americans liked it that way. When Parliament did pass laws that affected the colonies, the colonists sometimes ignored them. For example, they often smuggled goods they wanted from other nations instead of buying them from Britain. Colonists also elected local officials with a large degree of independence from London.

SONS OF LIBERTY

The Boston protests were led by a group of Massachusetts merchants and craftsmen called the Sons of Liberty. The group formed in Boston during the summer of 1765 and met in secret at first. Soon they numbered 2,000 men, and their protests drew much attention to the Patriot cause. By the end of 1765, Sons of Liberty groups existed in every colony.

But the relationship between the colonies and Great Britain grew tense after 1763. That year the British won the French and Indian War, in which Great Britain battled France for control of North America. Britain's victory gave it control of Canada and the eastern half of what became the United States. The war had been costly, and British officials demanded that colonists help pay for the future defense of the colonies.

In 1764 Parliament passed the American Revenue Act, known as the Sugar Act, which taxed goods including sugar, wine, coffee, and some types of cloth. The Sugar Act was the first law to raise new money in the colonies. Many merchants believed the new taxes would hurt their businesses.

The Americans cherished the British tradition that gave people the right to approve the taxes they paid. They did this through the representatives they elected to Parliament or colonial legislatures. The colonies, however, had no voting representatives in Parliament. More Americans began to protest against "taxation without representation."

In 1766 Parliament repealed the Stamp Act. But new taxes soon followed. The first of what came to be known as the Townshend Acts taxed glass, paint, paper, and tea imported from Britain. Some colonial merchants protested with a boycott of British goods. Boston was the center of the anger against the new laws. British officials there clamped down on smuggling. On June 10, 1768, the crew of a British warship seized a ship owned by Patriot merchant John Hancock, who was known for smuggling tea and molasses into the city. A crowd gathered to protest. Fists flew as the Americans beat up the British officials, leaving one of them bloody.

The violence in Boston led King George III to send British troops there. Soon they were camped in the heart of Boston. The residents shouted insults at the soldiers, known as "Redcoats" and "lobster backs" because of their bright red uniforms.

A MASSACRE IN BOSTON

At times citizens and soldiers fought. The worst violence came March 5, 1770. In front of the Custom House, British guard Private Hugh White was arguing with colonist Edward Garrick. Soon a crowd of angry colonists gathered in support of Garrick, hurling taunts of, "bloody lobster back" and "lousy rascal."

The Americans didn't just toss insults at the guard on duty that cold March night. The growing crowd pelted the soldier with chunks of ice. More soldiers rushed to the scene, and the crowd threw snowballs and sticks at them. Someone shouted, "Fire!" and

the soldiers fired their guns into the shouting mob. Three men fell dead to the ground. Two of the eight others who were wounded died later in what the Patriots called the Boston Massacre. Eight British soldiers and a captain were arrested and later tried on murder charges. All but two were acquitted.

The killings enraged some Boston Patriots, but the violence did not continue. Still, the residents' hatred of the troops simmered. It wouldn't be long before it reached a boiling point.

A RIOT OVER TEA

Most colonists drank tea every day. By 1770 Parliament had abolished all of the Townshend Acts but one—the tax on tea. In May 1773, though, Parliament passed the Tea Act. The law lowered

Eleven men were shot during the Boston Massacre.

the tax on tea, but allowed only the British East India Company to sell tea in the colonies. Even though colonists would pay less for the East India tea than for smuggled tea, they viewed the Tea Act as just one more example of British attempts to control their lives.

Several thousand people jammed into Boston's Old South Meeting House December 16, 1773, to discuss the fate of three loads of tea sitting in the harbor. The Patriots did not want the tea to come ashore. When it became clear the governor wouldn't let the ships leave until the tea was unloaded, Patriot leader Samuel Adams stood. "This meeting can do nothing more to save this country!" he shouted.

Adams' words were a signal to other Patriots in the crowd. That night dozens of men, some disguised as American Indians, boarded the ships and threw all the tea into the harbor.

In London an angry King George quickly responded to this "Boston Tea Party." He had Parliament pass several laws that punished Boston and the Massachusetts colony as a whole. They included shutting down the port of Boston and limiting local control of the government. Americans called these laws the Intolerable Acts.

Lawmakers called for a meeting to discuss how the colonies could act together to protest the new laws. Every colony except Georgia sent delegates to a meeting held in Philadelphia. This First Continental Congress called for another boycott of British goods if the laws punishing Massachusetts were not repealed.

FIRST SHOTS OF THE REVOLUTION

King George III and his advisers ignored the colonists' demands. In the colonies some members of Congress feared war might break out. But few colonists talked about independence from Great Britain. Most just wanted to protect the rights and freedoms they had always enjoyed as British citizens.

In Massachusetts, though, militia troops prepared for war. Their actions made royal governor Thomas Gage nervous. In September 1774 Gage ordered his troops to seize a large amount of gunpowder used by the militia. The incident sparked the militia to train men to serve as Minutemen—soldiers who were capable of fighting at a minute's notice.

Early in 1775 Gage received orders to arrest the Patriot leaders in Massachusetts. He also made plans to capture more of the local militias' weapons and supplies.

Gage put his plan into action the night of April 18. He sent troops to Concord, a town northwest of Boston. On horseback, Paul Revere and two other Patriots dashed ahead of the Redcoats to warn colonists along the way.

The next morning Minutemen in Lexington led by Captain John Parker waited for the advancing Redcoats. Parker had already decided that his men would not fire on the British unless the British fired first. When Redcoats came within sight, Parker told his men to back down. Some obeyed him. Others, like his cousin Jonas Parker, did not budge.

The April 19 battle raged on Concord Bridge and other sites.

Three British officers approached the Minutemen. One officer demanded, "Ye villains, ye rebels, disperse! Damn you, disperse!"

The scene quickly became chaotic. A gun fired, though no one knows who pulled the trigger. More gunfire quickly followed. Jonas Parker fell to the ground, hit by a British lead ball. He struggled to load his gun and fire back, but a British soldier stabbed him with a bayonet. Seven other Americans also died that morning.

The British then continued to Concord. The worst fighting of the day broke out in Concord and along the road back to Boston during the British retreat. Hiding in houses and behind fences, the Americans took deadly aim. They paid back the Redcoats for the deaths in Lexington, killing or wounding about 250 British troops. With the fighting that day, the Revolutionary War had begun.

A WAR FOR INDEPENDENCE

CH. 2

*M*ilitia members soon flocked to Massachusetts from other

colonies. Boston remained the center of the growing war. The

British sent more troops to the city, while American forces

surrounded it. In June Patriot leaders learned that the British

planned to take the hills outside Boston. The militia rushed to

nearby Breed's Hill and quickly put up a redoubt, a small fort made

of dirt and wood.

   The British attacked the American redoubt June 17. The fighting

was bloody. Two waves of British troops charged the fort and other

British soldiers charged three times in their quest to take Breed's Hill.

American defenses. The well-protected Americans cut down many Redcoats, driving them back. On their third charge, the British forced the Americans to flee.

The battle was named for nearby Bunker Hill, and in one sense, it was a British victory. But the British suffered more than 1,000 casualties. A Patriot writing in a Boston newspaper claimed, "Two more such actions will destroy your [the British] army."

WASHINGTON TAKES COMMAND

In Philadelphia the Second Continental Congress met to plan the war effort. Just before the Battle of Bunker Hill, Congress named George

Washington to lead the American soldiers. These troops included militias and a new national force called the Continental Army.

Washington arrived in Boston in July 1775. A militia officer for 20 years, Washington did not like what he saw. Despite the training of the Minutemen, most of the American forces weren't ready for serious battle. The camps were filthy and food sometimes rotted. Washington quickly made changes to clean the camps and improve discipline. Washington knew the Americans were fighting against a trained army. He wanted his forces to be at their best.

The Continental Army was carrying out a siege of Boston, trying to keep the British from receiving supplies. The siege continued into 1776. In early March Washington placed troops and cannons on the hills of Dorchester Heights, south of Boston. The British planned an attack on the hills, but it was stopped for several days by a storm. By the time the storm cleared, the British decided that the American position on the hills was too strong. The entire British force left the city March 17. To the Americans, it was a great victory. But the British would soon sail to New York City with an even larger army. Washington moved south to fight them there.

INDEPENDENCE

As the two armies headed for New York, the delegates of the Second Continental Congress were at work in Philadelphia. On June 7, 1776, the Congress began to discuss a resolution declaring independence from Great Britain. Five delegates were picked to write a declaration of independence.

Benjamin Franklin, Thomas Jefferson, Robert Livingston, John Adams, and Roger Sherman worked together on the Declaration of Independence.

Virginia lawyer Thomas Jefferson was the main author of the declaration. Jefferson and John Adams of Massachusetts briefly debated who should write the first draft. Adams insisted Jefferson do it, saying, "You can write ten times better than I can." "Well," Jefferson replied, "if you are decided, I will do as well as I can."

During the following days, Jefferson worked at a small wooden desk, searching for the right words for what would become a historic document. Jefferson asserted that all men are equal and have certain rights, and "among these are life, liberty, and the pursuit of happiness." The delegates approved the final version of Jefferson's declaration July 4. The 13 colonies were now the United States of America.

A BAD START

In August Washington's army and the British began a series of battles in New York. The campaign started badly for the Americans, with a major loss on Long Island. By November the British had taken New York City and several American forts just north of it. They had also captured more than 4,000 prisoners.

George Washington faced another problem as 1776 came to an end. Some of his soldiers had agreed to fight for just one year, and it was almost time for them to go home.

Despite his worries about his army, Washington saw a chance to finally score a major victory. The evening of December 25, he prepared his troops for a surprise attack on the Hessians, the German troops fighting for the British. As an icy storm raged

Washington led about 2,400 soldiers across the icy Delaware River on the way to Trenton, New Jersey.

around them, the Americans crossed the Delaware River. Around 8:00 a.m. the Americans arrived at the Hessian camp at Trenton, New Jersey. They killed about 20 Hessians, wounded about 100, and captured about 900, while losing only two of their own men.

After this victory, Washington was eager for another. But many of the soldiers were still preparing to go home. The commander asked if they would stay with him just one more month. More than 1,000 agreed to fight on.

Washington fought the British at Princeton, New Jersey, January 3. About 280 of the outnumbered British soldiers were killed, wounded, or missing, and the Americans captured British supplies. With the success in New Jersey, Americans' hopes rose. That spring thousands of men enlisted in the American army for terms of three years or more. But the Patriots still faced a long war.

THE OTHER AMERICANS

As the colonies came together to support Boston, some Americans rejected the Patriot cause. The Loyalists favored keeping their ties to Great Britain. Some Loyalists respected the wealth and power of Great Britain. Others thought the Americans had no right to rebel. Some simply disliked the dangers of war and how it affected their lives. The strongest Loyalists formed their own military companies and fought for the British against other Americans. Not surprisingly, Patriots hated the Loyalists who actively worked against independence. Loyalists in many states risked losing their property—or even their lives—if they spoke up too loudly for the British.

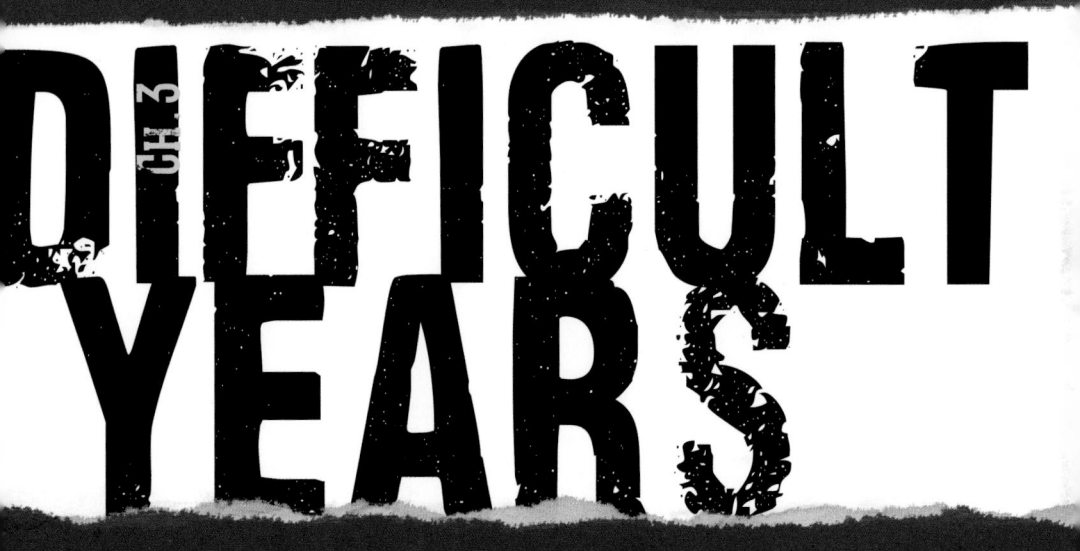

CH. 3 DIFFICULT YEARS

$\mathcal{I}$n spring 1777 British commander William Howe pulled his men

out of New Jersey and headed back to New York. His next target

was Philadelphia, the U.S. capital. Howe put his men on ships and

landed in Maryland. In September 1777 they marched north.

By now General Washington's army had grown to about 11,000

men, but the British Army still outnumbered it by about 7,000

troops. Washington's goal was to attack the British before they

reached Philadelphia.

American soldiers were routed at the Battle of Brandywine.

BRANDYWINE AND GERMANTOWN

On September 11 the Americans spread out along Brandywine
Creek in Pennsylvania. In a battle that lasted most of the day, the
British fooled the Americans by attacking with a small force in the
center, then sending a larger force to encircle the Americans from
the rear. The Americans suffered about twice as many casualties as
the British, who soon took Philadelphia.

In October the two armies clashed at nearby Germantown,
Pennsylvania. A heavy fog clung low over the battlefield, and
American troops struggled to carry out their generals' detailed battle
plan. The Americans once again lost, but Washington believed his
men had fought well against the better-trained British.

For the Patriots, the best news of 1777 came from New York. In two separate battles near Saratoga that fall, the Americans defeated a British force that was moving south from Canada. Several heroes emerged during the battles, though least among them might have been the U.S. commander, Horatio Gates. At times Gates was slow to move his larger force against the British troops under General John Burgoyne. Another American general, Benedict Arnold, argued with the commander about what to do. At one point he defied Gates' order to stay in camp.

At both Saratoga battles, Arnold bravely led charges against the British. While attacking a British redoubt, Arnold had his horse

Daniel Morgan and his riflemen played an important role in the victories at Saratoga.

HERO AND TRAITOR

Benedict Arnold is remembered today as a terrible traitor. He turned against the Patriot cause in 1779 to help the British. But Arnold also had been one of the bravest generals on the American side. Throughout the war Arnold believed he didn't receive the rewards he deserved for his heroic service, which led to his leaving the Patriot side. After the war Arnold lived for a time in Canada and then settled in England, where he died a poor man in 1801.

shot from underneath him. "Rush on, my brave boys!" he called to his men, and they did, dodging bullets to take the redoubt. Also crucial at both battles were Colonel Daniel Morgan and his expert riflemen. With their second victory, the Americans took almost 6,000 prisoners. The success at Saratoga led France to join the war against Great Britain. The French had already been sending the Americans money and supplies. Now they would fight the British at sea and begin to send men to help the Americans.

A DIFFICULT WINTER

Washington and his troops next moved to Valley Forge, Pennsylvania, to spend the winter. Tired from a tough campaign, the men began building small wooden huts there in December 1777.

As the winter went on, the troops battled the cold and disease while their bellies often ached for food. The soldiers were living on little more than "fire cakes" made of flour and water. The cry of

"No meat! No meat!" rang through the camp. In his headquarters Washington worried his army might not make it through the winter.

Keeping warm was another problem. The huts weren't sturdy enough to keep out the cold wind. Many soldiers were wearing rags. As many as 3,000 soldiers were dead by spring.

BETTER DAYS

Things began to look up for Washington's army in March. Army engineers began repairing the roads and bridges between the town of Lancaster and the camp, which allowed wagons of food to reach Valley Forge.

But the soldiers were still undisciplined and poorly trained. That changed with the arrival of Friedrich von Steuben. The professional soldier from the German kingdom of Prussia was skilled in the best European methods of keeping men organized during battle. Steuben

Friedrich von Steuben (right) trained the Americans to be skilled fighters.

personally trained a small number of Americans, and they then taught the other soldiers at Valley Forge.

They had their first chance to use their new skills in June 1778. The British left Philadelphia to return to New York. Some of Washington's troops waited for them at Monmouth Courthouse, New Jersey. On the sweltering hot morning of June 28, the battle there started badly for the Americans. They outnumbered the British, but American General Charles Lee seemed confused about what to do.

Washington arrived at the battle and was shocked to see his men retreating. Washington then rallied the troops to form a defensive line. Throughout the day the British attacked and the Americans held them off, helped by the accurate pounding of their artillery. The fighting ended as evening approached, with the Americans suffering about 500 casualties and the British about 1,100. During the night the British pulled out and continued on to New York.

The Battle of Monmouth Courthouse showed the increasing skill of the American troops. But the war for independence was now more than three years old. Many Americans had not expected it to go on so long. Still they were willing to fight on, as the main fighting shifted to the South.

FINAL VICTORY

CH.4

*I*n December 1778 British warships sailed up the Savannah River and seized the city of Savannah, Georgia. By early 1779 the rest of Georgia was under British control. The next year the British began a siege of Charleston, South Carolina. The city fell in May 1780, and about 5,000 Americans were taken prisoner.

The war in the South soon turned into a bloody civil war of sorts. Large numbers of Loyalists turned their weapons against American Patriots. American General Nathanael Greene saw that the Loyalists and Patriots "pursue one another with the most relentless fury, killing and destroying each other wherever they meet."

Nathanael Greene (center, on horseback) became a strong Patriot leader.

A DIFFICULT START

Support for the Patriots in the Carolinas rose or fell depending on how well they did on the battlefield. The fighting often did not go well for the Americans. For a time Horatio Gates commanded the Americans in South Carolina. But unlike the victories at Saratoga, Gates' forces lost badly at the Battle of Camden. Many of the survivors went home rather than fight again.

The Americans did better in South Carolina fighting in small units. These groups ranged in size from 50 to 500 men. Francis Marion was one of the bold and daring men who led the guerrillas against the enemy. Marion was known as the Swamp Fox for his skill in avoiding British troops.

In response, the British sometimes robbed or destroyed the homes of Patriots. Patriot Eliza Wilkinson feared for her life when Redcoats on horseback thundered up to her sister's South Carolina home. Pistols and swords drawn, the British tore through the house, stealing jewelry and clothing. Wilkinson called the Redcoats "inhuman monsters."

SOUTHERN SUCCESS

After Gates' defeat at Camden, Nathanael Greene took over as the American commander in the South. Greene had helped improve the supply system during the hard winter at Valley Forge.

Greene split his army in two. Daniel Morgan led a group of cavalry and other skilled soldiers, while Greene took the rest of the men. In January 1781 Morgan's forces met part of the British army at a spot in South Carolina where cows once grazed. At the Battle of the Cowpens, Morgan formed the Americans into several lines. The

AFRICAN-AMERICANS IN THE REVOLUTION

During battles in the South and across the country, African-Americans fought next to whites. Some of the black American soldiers were slaves, and their masters received money for their services. Others were free blacks such as Lemuel Haynes. The Massachusetts Minuteman fought in several battles of the Revolution. In 1776 Haynes wrote against slavery: "Even an African, has equally as good a right to his liberty in common with Englishmen."

sharpshooters were in front, followed by Continental troops, while the cavalry soldiers were at the rear.

When the British soldiers charged, the Americans retreated. The Redcoats scattered as they chased the Americans, which allowed the American cavalry to ride in and swiftly attack. As the fighting went on, Morgan rode up to his troops. Flashing his sword, he said, "Give them one more fire and the day is ours." The Americans kept firing, and the British quickly surrendered.

Greene then joined Morgan, and the combined force fought the British at Guilford Courthouse in North Carolina. The Americans finally retreated, but the British paid a high price for the victory, with more than 500 casualties to the Americans' 250.

Lord Charles Cornwallis, the British commander, decided to head north to Virginia. Fighting was already under way there during the first part of 1781. French officer Marquis de Lafayette led both American and French troops. The British had several thousand troops in the state, which were joined by Cornwallis' soldiers in May. After several small battles, Cornwallis set up camp in Yorktown on the York River.

The French had sent thousands of soldiers to help the Americans, and powerful warships were also on the way. In August Washington decided the French and American forces would attack the British in Virginia. Together the two allies had about twice as many men as the British. Meanwhile, French ships kept British aid from reaching Cornwallis by sea.

Washington began a siege of Yorktown. The largest cannons began firing on the British October 9 and kept firing for a week. The British shot back as well, and one officer was concerned for Washington's safety as he watched the fighting.

"Sir, you are too much exposed here, had you not better step a little back?" the officer asked.

Washington replied to the aide, "If you are afraid, you have liberty to step back." The commander, though, did not move.

Meanwhile, American soldiers dug trenches closer and closer to the British lines. French and American troops captured two British redoubts October 14. From there they would be able to do even more damage with their big guns. Three days later a single British officer waved a white cloth at the Americans. Cornwallis was ready to surrender. The final agreement between Washington and Cornwallis was reached October 19.

WOMEN AT WAR

Patriot women did important work during the war. They ran farms and businesses and collected money for clothing. Some traveled with the troops to feed the men and nurse the wounded. A few even fought the British. One of these female soldiers was Massachusetts schoolteacher Deborah Samson.

In May 1782 21-year-old Samson disguised herself as a man named Robert Shurtliff and enlisted in the American army. She fought for the next 18 months alongside the male soldiers and was wounded in at least one battle. When her gender was discovered, the Army gave her an honorable discharge in October 1783. She later received a small pension from the state of Massachusetts for her service.

News of the American victory at Yorktown reached Great Britain in November. The fighting still went on, but British leaders were no longer certain they could win. Early in 1782 Parliament agreed to end the war. Several Patriot leaders were already in Europe to discuss a peace treaty, which was signed September 3, 1783. The Treaty of Paris granted the Americans their independence.

Across the country Americans celebrated peace and independence. They had won a war that Washington had called "a defense of all that is dear and valuable in life."

A British soldier waving a white flag signified the British surrender at Yorktown.

INDEX

Adams, John, 15
Adams, Samuel, 9
Arnold, Benedict, 20–21

battles
    Brandywine, 19
    Bunker Hill, 12–13
    Camden, 25, 26
    Cowpens, the, 26–27
    Germantown, 19
    Guilford Courthouse, 27
    Lexington and
        Concord, 10–11
    Monmouth
        Courthouse, 23
    Princeton, 17
    Saratoga, 20–21, 25
    Trenton, 16–17
    Yorktown, 27–29
Boston Massacre, 7–8

Cornwallis, Lord Charles,
    27, 28

Declaration of Independence,
    14–15

First Continental
    Congress, 9, 10
French aid, 21, 27, 28
French and Indian War, 6

Gage, Thomas, 10
Gates, Horatio, 20, 25, 26
George III, King, 7, 9, 10
Greene, Nathanael, 24, 26–27

Hancock, John, 7
Haynes, Lemuel, 26

Jefferson, Thomas, 15

Lafayette, Marquis de, 27
laws
    Intolerable Acts, 9
    Stamp Act, 4–5, 7
    Sugar Act, 6
    Tea Act, 8–9
    Townshend Acts, 7, 8
Loyalists, 17, 24

Marion, Francis, 25
militia, 10, 12–13, 14
Minutemen, 10–11, 14
Morgan, Daniel, 21, 26–27

Parker, John, 10
Parker, Jonas, 10–11
Parliament, 5, 6–7, 8, 9, 29
protests, 4, 5, 6–7, 9
    Boston Tea Party, 9

Revere, Paul, 10

Samson, Deborah, 28
Second Continental Congress,
    13, 14
smuggling, 5, 7, 9
Sons of Liberty, 6
surrender, 27, 28–29

taxes, 4–5, 6–7, 8–9
Treaty of Paris, 29

Valley Forge, Pennsylvania,
    21–23, 26
von Steuben, Friedrich, 22–23

Washington, George, 13–14,
    16–17, 18, 19, 21–23,
    27–28, 29

GLOSSARY

ARTILLERY—large guns that are usually moved on wheels and require more than one person to load and fire

BAYONET—metal blade attached to the end of a musket

BOYCOTT—refuse to buy, as a protest against an unpopular act or policy

CAMPAIGN—series of battles fought in one region

CASUALTIES—soldiers killed, wounded, missing, or taken prisoner during a battle

CAVALRY—soldiers who fight on horseback

GUERRILLAS—fighters who carry out small attacks and then blend in with the local population

INTOLERABLE—so harsh or bad that it cannot be accepted

MILITIA—groups of citizens who have been organized to fight as a group but who are not professional soldiers

REDOUBT—a small fort built quickly, often made out of dirt and rocks

SIEGE—a military effort to surround a location and prevent the people there from receiving food or supplies

TRAITOR—someone who works against the interests of his or her country

INTERNET SITES

Use FactHound to find Internet sites related to this book. All of the sites on FactHound have been researched by our staff.

Here's all you do:

Visit *www.facthound.com*

Type in this code: 9780756545703

TIMELINE

1763
The British end their war with France and Spain, gaining new lands in North America

1764
Parliament passes the Sugar Act

1765
Americans protest the Stamp Act

1766
Parliament repeals the Stamp Act

1767
The Townshend Acts place new taxes on the colonies

1768
British officials seize the ship of Boston merchant John Hancock, leading to violence; the British government sends troops to the city

1770
British troops clash with Boston residents, killing five in what the Americans call the Boston Massacre and the British call the Boston Riot

1777
January 3: The Americans defeat the British at Princeton, New Jersey

July: A British army marching south from Canada takes Fort Ticonderoga, New York

September: The British win at Brandywine, Pennsylvania, and then take the American capital of Philadelphia; the British suffer heavy losses at the first battle of Saratoga

October: The Americans surprise British forces at Germantown but are driven back; the American victory at the second battle of Saratoga forces the British to turn over 6,000 prisoners and leads to France's joining the war against the British

1778
June: The British leave Philadelphia for New York and clash with the Americans at Monmouth Courthouse, New Jersey

December: The British invade Georgia

1779
June: Spain declares war on Britain

October: American and French soldiers stage a failed attack on British-held Savannah, Georgia

1773

Boston residents throw crates of tea into the harbor to protest the Tea Act

1774

To punish Massachusetts for the tea protest, Parliament passes a series of laws called the Intolerable Acts in the colonies and the Coercive Acts in Britain; the First Continental Congress meets

1775

April 19: The Battles of Lexington and Concord begin the Revolutionary War

June: George Washington is named commander of the Continental Army; the British suffer heavy losses during their victory at the Battle of Bunker Hill

1776

July 4: The colonies declare their independence from Britain

August 27: The British win the Battle of Long Island

December 26: Washington launches a surprise attack on British forces in Trenton

1780

May: The British take Charleston, South Carolina

August 16: The Americans lose badly at Camden, South Carolina

October 7: The British suffer heavy losses at Kings Mountain, South Carolina

1781

January 17: Americans win the Battle of the Cowpens in South Carolina

March 15: At Guilford Courthouse, North Carolina, the British drive off the Americans but suffer heavy casualties

September: A combined U.S.-French force reaches Virginia and begins a siege of General Cornwallis' forces at Yorktown

October 19: Cornwallis surrenders at Yorktown

1782

Parliament votes to end the war against America

1783

The British and Americans sign the Treaty of Paris on September 3, which officially gives the United States its independence

Select Bibliography

Boatner, Mark M. III. *Encyclopedia of the American Revolution*. 3rd ed. Mechanicsburg, Pa.: Stackpole Books, 1994.

Commager, Henry Steele, and Richard B. Morris, eds. *The Spirit of Seventy-Six: The Story of the American Revolution As Told by Participants*. New York: Da Capo Press, 1995.

The Economics of the American Revolutionary War. 20 April 2012. www://eh.net/encyclopedia/article/baack.war.revolutionary.us

Fleming, Thomas J. *Liberty!: The American Revolution*. New York: Viking, 1997.

Hibbert, Christopher. *Redcoats and Rebels: The American Revolution Through British Eyes*. New York: Norton, 1990.

Middlekauff, Robert. *The Glorious Cause: The American Revolution 1763–1789*. New York: Oxford University Press, 1982.

Pearson, Michael. *Those Damned Rebels: The American Revolution as Seen Through British Eyes*. New York: Putnam, 1972.

Rhodehamel, John, ed. *The American Revolution: Writings from the War of Independence*. New York: The Library of America, 2001.

Weintraub, Stanley. *Iron Tears: America's Battle for Freedom, Britain's Quagmire: 1775–1783*. New York: Free Press, 2005.

Further Reading

Catel, Patrick. *Key People of the Revolutionary War*. Chicago: Heinemann Library, 2011.

Gregory, Josh. *The Revolutionary War*. New York: Children's Press, 2012.

Kent, Deborah. *The American Revolution: From Bunker Hill to Yorktown*. Berkeley Heights, N.J.: Enslow, 2011.

Schanzer, Rosalyn. *George vs. George: The American Revolution As Seen from Both Sides*. Washington, D.C.: National Geographic, 2004.